# Misadventure

RICHARD MEIER lives in north London
with his wife, daughter and son.
*Misadventure* is his first book.

D1419843

# Contents

# Misadventure

# Winter morning

Shyly coated in greys, blacks, browns –
to keep us out of sight of the cold –
we weren't expecting *this* this morning: sun

and shadows, like a summer's evening, like summer
teasing. And not quite under the shelter on
the northbound platform, an old man, the sun

behind him, just his crown ablaze; and heading
southbound, a woman inching ever nearer
the platform edge, the light a tear

across her midriff, ribcage, shoulders, closer
and closer that dearest thing, completeness,
all her darkness light at the one time.

# Misadventure

Nothing again to show for his week's work
he rises early on the Saturday vowing
*I will achieve one thing today*
and drives up to the plant-hire by the station.

Back home and all set up, he squeezes the handle
of the high-pressure patio cleaner. There,
to his surprise, a fat dash where he'd fired.
He squeezes it again, more firmly; draws

a line so clean, so neat, from one side to
the other, he's a Moses, then from slab
to slab he paces, making sure to judge
the distance to perfection: not too close –

the jet, he learns, is strong enough to unpick
mortar – not too far lest it merely tongue
the surface. Finished, he stands to admire
the patio newly-laid, the shining stone.

But seeing his mud-stippled feet, he turns
the nozzle on them and – amazed – beholds
a brand new pair of tennis shoes emerge,
with snowy laces; then puts one foot up,

like someone being shod, to clean his sole,
each pimple and impression, then the other,
then sets about his shins, his calves – he's soaked
anyway – to purge dirt from each trouser-leg

and bellywards, as if the vigour might
unlard him, then across his heart, as if
the keenness of the water could absolve it;
and higher, to the brain, its dump of dud

connections where, quite reasonably, he places
the nozzle in his mouth and pulls the trigger

# Fabric

She was kind – still I wished I hadn't called her
(we'd been out together only twice)
in those first moments after I'd been told
my grandmother had died. We'd just been chatting,
yet it felt wrong putting such old,
experienced feelings next to ones so fresh.

At midnight on our third and final date
I stepped inside her Edwardian conversion
to find a stripped-pine, bookless space complete
with kitchen like an operating theatre,
bathroom more a boutique marble quarry
and something too near horror at the thought

that she could live like this, unstoried, bar
a silk dressing gown, floral and antique,
I noticed as I closed the bedroom door
and grasped, then, like the answer to all grief,
all absence, till the sleeve ran through my fingers
like fine, unsunned sand as I reached for her.

# For a bridge suicide

From four, six, eight feet, maybe even ten,
water's a giving, all-embracing thing.

Above that, it begins to darken, starts
to slap, to harden, till by fifty or sixty

limbs get broken. Still, even at that height,
you feel if you just got your entry right

you could elicit softness, could slip in ...
And yet, for all that, there's a point

when water's transformation is complete,
a point at which the whole of the earth's surface

is uniformly unforgiving. As
she neared the top of the bridge's central stanchion

this was the point she recognised. And let go

# The promise

Unoccupied, unbothered, it lay back –
the famous Finnish plywood armchair –
like an easy throne. In books I'd long admired
its elbowed arm-rests, the kinked seat unscrolling
at either end; here though, in the flesh,
the birch-ply shocked me, looking so inert,
all dull and sunless, like some demonstration
of what the years can do to an idea.
And what an idea it had been, this mixing
of curve and coolness; what an end, such promise
of give, of comfort, undelivered.

# Crocuses

All year we breathe the earth before exhaling.
And what comes out is colour –

buttercup, purple, lilac, white –
and all the vowels.

It's how we make the world,
this tone, this note we hold

until it kills us, till
our first-born come, the daffodils.

Look at them with their round-mouthed, plainsong faces –
open so, such anyhowness

# The top field

One thing only could we give them: sleep.
Not that we knew that, when the stable-girls
accepted, saying *OK, you can fetch*
*the horses from the top field in the morning*
and booked themselves a lie-in. No, that night,
and as we picked our way up through the woods
at half-six on that Friday, we were chosen,
and the world with its jodhpured, confident thighs
seemed closer: here was life, we three felt, leading
the line of steaming and half-sleeping horses
down from the mist-filled field towards the stables.

But as we reached the last turn, where the path
widened, a pulse ran through the horses,
inexperience, or breakfast, bowling
them on, and galloping now, and then gone,
one big bolus of horse bottle-necking
the open gate, some slipping through though – one,
a chestnut pony, like an upright piano,
skating into the far wall which collapsed
matter-of-factly, softly, the horse lifting
his head to see three sprinting girls as he
lay dying 'from internal injuries',
we would learn, back at school for the spring term.

# Walking near Arundel

Chalk and mud. Fields littered with flint.
A river, some rushes, a tan landscape

and *There, over there!* the black and steel
of a heron's elegance. And the breeze,

resisting us, newly-fleshing us as
we stand silenced on this hillside ...

How exactly the wind fits our faces.

# Sky sports

The gods, who can *see* feelings, love
to watch us as we foist emotions –
hard ones, largely – onto others.
Imagine paint-ball but with shame,
or envy, rather than emulsion:

so the gods will turn their gaze
on certain characters in offices,
on mealtimes in some marriages,
on the blank mornings of a new mother;
or rather on their victims who may

or may not wonder why they feel
stupid, say, or dirty, worthless, while
the gods whoop, marvelling at this deft
gift of ours for shifting misery
that makes for such great viewing. Kills some even.

# The Feeder

In what for you was something of a departure,
you bought me this lovely, if demanding, gift
for Christmas. After lunch I held it aloft
by various trees and fence-posts till we thought

we'd found its ideal spot, so we could watch.
Or I could, since you'd left me by the time,
an untouched fortnight later, I first noticed
the seed level had dropped. Bit by bit

it would fall daily and, since one tense wren
was all I'd glimpsed come near the thing, I saw
how lightly there you'd always been; and how
it could sustain me, your being here alone.

# Psychotherapy

Across the way, a paver with a maul:
an old-style wooden one he wields
as if he's chopping something

or else straddles croquet-fashion
to thump, to nudge, the flagstones level;
blows you'd think must surely split them.

But by the look of this thing's head –
dented and mashed, a real veteran –
it's known meaner collisions and come off worst.

And yet it can still speak with rock,
can still find the reason there,
some kindness in the stone, the give.

# Opening and closing of the double-glazed man

Mean,
this man,

shut, unosmotic,
shocking then, shocking,

the scene this lunchtime,
how he unsealed, how he broke open ...

And near the silence from which we watched him,
a sense of vast rebalancing

as if, of the two – the universe
and he – he were the denser,

pressure flowing who knows whence
in glad, baroque incontinence:

an annual rainfall in an hour,
a cactus letting go to flower

till equilibrium
returned, and shame,

and then
that from-an-upstairs-window look of his again.

## Domestic

The birds are here, of course, before us: one
and then another, then a dozen darting
down from the branches to the garden
for this fierce inspection of the ground.

Until a sound, some movement behind glass,
returns them – like riches lifted up
in outstretched arms and scattered –
back up to the trees. Poor things, how close

we live to their world, never more
than a stone's throw away; how fragile, all
that's crammed there, in between the fear, the hunger:
brickwork, windows, distance, thought, what have you.

# Sea Palling

Lee side of the dune,
everything worth protecting:

the plain; a pair of rusting
horses; cabins none alike.

Windward side, the waves'
soft bombing. And the dune,

this arm round England's exposed
shoulder? Firmer, since

the flood; sterner with
its concrete splints.

Can one revert,
it wonders – it has time –

to something of a looser love,
still watchful, more alive?

How, the dune wants to know
(and it has seen the sea

do rage and trust turned flotsam),
does one become un-sickened, un-dismayed?

# Tables for two

Sometimes we eat at a broad, thick farmhouse table,
with drawers above our laps
where cold, bone-handled knives lie waiting.

Sometimes we eat at a bird-legged, bistro table,
knowing one slip
could send everything crashing.

Sometimes at my parents' chipped formica table
then vast enough
for my brother and me to play ping-pong on it,

and sometimes at an antique rosewood one
which has this central piece
that opens out of nowhere like it's flowering

# Renunciation

Times when he feels his mother must be worried
he will say, to help, *That must be worrying* ...

Times when he senses in her latent sadness,
he will venture *That must be upsetting* ...

Today, though, as he left the hospital –
she was staying with his dad a little

longer – he felt as though a faith fell from him,
this gospel of his of authenticity,

his mother there, alone and knowing it,
afraid, and feeling that too, the lift doors closing.

# Three weeks to go

I was sitting, as I often do
at lunchtime, in the burialground off Church Street
(there's not much green in Acton) when in came

a woman with a guide-dog. I assumed
she'd sit down on a bench and that her old,
ruckled, paperback-yellow Lab would lie

beside her; but instead, she stood and unleashed
her dog who shot off like a puppy, dribbling
through the headstones, scooting round the yews,

the oak trees. As you know, I am a tethered,
youthless man. But the way that that dog danced —
that's how I feel about marrying you.

# Moment

That moment in a wedding –
the sense of cresting, as the goodwill wells –

say one could translate that into sight
you'd see, perhaps, two people side by side –

there in the newfound centre of the world –
in front of them a mirror and one more behind

in which they find reflected first themselves

then all the couples who have stood as frank as they do –
all the marrying kind – arranged along

love's entire length in one pulsating line
that, captured in the language of the heart,

feels like a cresting, as the goodwill wells –
that moment in a wedding.

# That we might have a garden

It was late, almost too late, by the time
I knelt to part the gravel with my hands
and peered at what lay underneath. *Look!*

I called, as you searched for the rubble sacks,
the shovel, and we stared at it, this substance,
rich as anything, a dark, brown butter.

And then we launched in, shifting spadeload upon
heaped spadeload, till we'd twenty, thirty bags
of worthless coin stacked on the patio

and stood there in the gold light of the kitchen,
silent with responsibility,
looking at a new earth.

# Building Matilda

I — IN TIME

Back when the future, I mean *children*,
was something which, in time, we'd choose,
we'd mooch round farmers' markets, antiques fairs
and – though okay for food, fine for furniture –
would buy odd things from stalls, almost from pity.

Now that it will not come, the future,
we mimic *living* while we wait behind
our hopes, laid out like stalls to coax them
to us, to browse, should they but choose
our fine, well-furnished home, as much from pity.

## II — ROULETTE

*Put it on a number*, you smile, catching
me chart the pattern of the last ten goes.
Funny to end up here, at the casino,
the first night of this break we can't afford,
but need, we feel, before the IVF.

Nine of the last ten being red, I plump
for black: first two chips (red though, damn), then four
(fuck, red again), now six (no prizes), then –
all in – our last eight chips, and watch the ball
race round and round the wall of the roulette wheel,

so shiny I can see you, smaller,
in that nightshirt the same cut as your dress,
emerging from the bathroom one month hence
to show me, by your look, that everything
is lost, or else not lost at all, but yes, but yes …

III – THE SCIENCE BIT

Say that what makes you female is a flame
then what these hormones, these injections do

is turn that flame down low, so low
the slightest breath and it would be extinguished;

and all the time these chemicals control
the essence of you, you are null, an absence,

before a fresh course pours on paraffin
and *whoosh!* you conflagrate until, from somewhere,

ten eggs appear, collected to be mixed
with what the male produces in a small

white room before some pictures of a blonde
who looks completely up for it, and not there.

## IV — Portrait of a woman in the first weeks of pregnancy

Not a study in consolation —

but a woman holding out a slate before her,
a slate upon which sits a drop of mercury,
a drop that wants to stick together,
wants to come apart ... A woman who

stands on a boat of some kind, running
at every pitch, scrambling at every yaw,
to stop the drop from slipping, spilling,
lest, if it should fall, it would become
a million grief-filled molecules breathed in for ever more.

A woman who, after a good while of this,
is starting to get the gist, to grin.

A woman who may even be dancing

## v – ROUTINE SCAN

Since we've seen a heart
(at six weeks), and an eye
(at nine), I don't suppose

this twelve-week check will top that,
I half-think, as across
the screen swims one hand, then

another, like five, ten
of the tiniest light-bulbs
ever manufactured, *on*.

vi − Section

Our side of this wind-break/surgical screen,
a man and half a woman sheltering.

Radio 3 gusts through the theatre: *Brahms*
I pronounce, unsure, trying to distract us

from the powerlessness. That, and the hope
we're scared to open. So we stay low till,

in the finale (*Dvorak*, it transpires),
a quickening and a lifting up, and we −

winners after all − reach out, called, to take
hold of our flailing, purple cup, our prize.

VII – PETAL

Not a word I've used for anyone
before. And not particular, or funny,
like *molecule*, say, as your mother calls you.

Matilda, *petal* – little love-evoker –
I stand above your sleep-surrendered soul,
or else pull outsize grins you'll learn, I fear,

your father's not exactly famous for,
all teary, like a man half-cut,
but so, so sober. And completely yours.

VIII – First birthday

Who would have thought that as I held
the sides of the inflatable 'house' we'd bought our daughter –
and which had lain, a good hour earlier

before I'd started on it with the foot-pump,
a slick of plastic on the floor – I'd feel the structure
right itself in my grasp, then lift a little

and raise my hands so that the arms I'd lifted
to help it up, to realise its form, its nature,
seemed guy-ropes tethering it to the ground.

# Early learning

He's had his go, so now his sister
gets to be the one being chased
and gets to be the one who's caught
and reassembled by mum's embrace.

He tries to watch, to wait quietly
and for ten, twenty seconds keeps still
but then proceeds to squeal and scamper
pretending he's being chased as well

and, even though his mother blanks him,
carries on – since what else is there? –
and might have never stopped had she
not saved him with a chase-like gesture;

and calmed now, back in her arms,
he studies her for recognition
of their shared fib – grin at the ready –
as if it were all done with, nothing

## Compos mentis

The breeze leans into the side of the home,
the gentlest of reminders. We gaze outside.
*Aren't the leaves dropping early this year?*
my grandmother moots for the umpteenth time.

Summoning a *Hmm*, I quiz her again
about the people here, the food, but she cuts in –
*I'm sure they're dropping much earlier this year* –
making it clear this is no time for small-talk.

# Write about what you know

Maybe, in those days, I assumed the shed
would be the stronger. Or the ceanothus
would prove accommodating. Well, whichever,

within two years, the shrub, a tree really,
had pushed up, through and over its new neighbour
the way – it not being in its nature to go

around – a tank might a car in a war-zone.
Such single-mindedness had had a price though,
left its trunk twisted, listing. Then, each spring,

it flowered as bluely, yet with fewer blooms
and for less long. And when this year it fizzed
a few days only, I found I didn't need

my axe, nor handsaw hardly, just my hands
to fell the entire desiccated thing,
to fold it inside the urn of one sack.

# A hopeless gardener thanks his wife

So hopeless, in fact, that when the meadowseed
they'd put down proffered some green stubble
eight or nine days later he would stare
at it dumbfounded. And though he felt sad
when the 'meadow' grew up somewhat flowerless
(this despite the riot on the packet)
it was no surprise. *I'm sorry,* he'll sigh,
*it's not so much a husband you escort*
*about our garden, these days, as a patient*,
so faithless is he that the passionflower'll
survive till she has shown him it unfurl
around her twine; faithless, till she points out
how far they've spanned that blank, uncloseable
width of fence, the jasmine and the honeysuckle.

# Relative

*In the sixties, of course, no one ever*
*said no*, he starts for my benefit.
One by one his mates chip in,
backing him up, flush with examples,
staggered still how easy it was then.
Fresh out of college, I sit there nodding,
mock-agog at my glum uncle
and cocky enough, then, to dismiss
what he deems the closest to paradise
you could ever come. *Just imagine,*
he marvels – *everywhere you walked,*
*everywhere you looked, work, work, work.*

# Blackberrying in a time of recession

*You can't eat those ones, darling,*
I tell Matilda as she tries,
as she tried yesterday, to pick the last
blackberries at the bottom of the garden,

these hard, dull garnets carrying on
as if warmth lasts indefinitely;
those the bushes seem prepared to lose –
opting to fruit while there's the slightest sun.

It's mid-October – the best times have gone.
And it is simple and yet hard
to tell my toddling, student daughter
why some can't now ripen, won't now shine.

# On the road out of Roussillon

I bought an ochre tile with *24*
glazed on it, as if I still deemed 'home'
the flat I'd been mugged outside a week before,

and waited while the potter packaged it much
too cautiously, I felt, then cycled on
to the next town. But locking up,

a gust from nowhere scragged my bike and spilled
the contents of my saddle-bag: new phone,
new wallet (slim still as a child),

this tile. It lay in fragments, bubble-wrapped,
the meaning shattered. Me and it undone,
courier and artefact.

# Conditions

Waking now and then, in the small hours,
I listen to the dark to make sure you're
still breathing. Which, of course,

you are, you are. And here, beside
the bed, the glucose gel I'd need
to give you should you sleep too deeply, too completely.

Ours is a quiet neighbourhood
yet in my head some mob-boss-god
exacts protection night and day.

And with some part of me – some part
less quiet, less ashamed, in exchange
for which perhaps we'll be let be – I pay.

# The tour-guide

The way her voice would crumple, horrified
afresh by each fact, story, she recounted,
brought us even closer to the detail:

the meanness of the breeze,
the ridge at Passchendaele
you'd barely notice even on a bicycle.

Great-grandchild of an Aussie sapper
and a Belgian farm-hand, she had volunteered
for this, this daily sacrifice we felt

appalled to witness and yet grateful for;
and which we left her to, our stricken Atlas
carrying not the world but its pity.

# Maddened by this world

I made another,

one where when I said
*Are we OK?*, you didn't shake your head,
but smiled instead

and we went on. A world quite similar
to this one, yet where it's less seldom summer;
a second home, a

luxury item I can ill
afford, but need to be there till
that moment, should it come, when I'll

forget I ever owned
it (with that sense of what has gone
existing in some way or other,

spinning on)

# We'll always have Paris

Broke, almost, I came home by coach.
I'd gone there with my girlfriend of three years,
then left her three days after meeting you.

You liked me but I didn't move you, couldn't,
not as some could, and we slept together twice,
to prove it, in the studio I'd moved to

and where (there was a piano but no heating)
I'd sit, mid-Chopin, sobbing hoarse, raw sobs
I didn't know I had inside me. Outside

Calais, the traffic thickened as we passed
a burnt-out pile-up, maybe twenty vehicles.

*C'est quelque chose*, our driver said to the guy
in the toll-booth, *vraiment quelque chose*.

# White out

No time more apt to leave you than midwinter.

The way the snow takes over, grips
us in its coterie of terms –
*settle*, *treacherous*, *black ice*, *grit* –
so it is with you.

The way that we respond to snow –
the more experienced the warier –
so, I'm afraid, to you.

And like you, too, the way –
I see now after all these blinded years –
the stuff seems so substantial
yet represents, in truth, a dearth.

Of colour, contrast, purchase, warmth.

# Still

Waiting for the bath to finish running,
I catch us both in your full-length mirror

and freeze, aged twelve again, faced with
that shot of a man and a woman

my biology primer
would openly fall open on.

How it's stayed with me – the hang
of the arms. Those clothed expressions.

# Please collect all winter coats

*(from a notice in the local drycleaners' window)*


In single file, they wait the summer out,
        clean, forgotten.
Housed with them, in the silence of their folds,
        a notion (autumn)
now unthinkable. Late August, light
        lengthens, goldens –
and so starts the reclaiming, coat by coat.

# To a new teacher

Between the old job, which half-killed you, and
the new career you've planned

so long now, you have summered
half with Homer, half with the mud

of our young garden. *What I love*
you'll say, typically, *is how he'll give*

*each warrior, however briefly mentioned,*
*all his gaze, his whole attention,*

then lead me outside and straight onto
what's been uprooted, what's been planted.

You who've camped out on the outskirts of
your own life long enough,

you who know how hard
they often are to tell apart –

the living, the
unliving thing –

you're leaving Limbo now, in your own style.
Simply, amply, with your book, your trowel.

# Canute explains

What narked me, watching England
dwindle from the boat,
that first time I'd invaded,
wasn't so much being forced
to retreat, so much as
it meant missing the looks
of those who would arrive
victorious at that shoreline
only to find their brothers
bloodied and sobbing on
the sand, scattered around them –
like the leftovers from
some outrageous banquet –
ear lobes, noses, hands.

Three years later, and king now,
I got married. Odd
how we clicked, Emma and I,
she being the old king's widow.
Still, she liked me, liked
teaching me what she'd learnt
about the country (she
was a foreigner too).
To my amazement, and hers,
I got into all things
English. Even the food.

How many hundreds, thousands,
must have been hoping peacetime
would suit me too? And when
it palled – anathema
to rage, this deep, dear fund
of rage – I found myself
conquering Norway and chunks
of Sweden till there I was,
aged thirty, with the vastest
empire ever, immeasurably
unhappy.

        Hard,
isn't it, to say where
or when they start, our changes
of heart, these softenings?


Much later though, in Rome
(what a place!, *warm* for one thing –
the Pope himself had asked
me there) and some way through
not so much a conversion,
more a kind of becoming,
I wrote that letter home –
'To the English people':
apologising for all
the wars and shortages,

the maiming and the rape,
for the galaxy of taxes.
Everyone loved me then.

Only that made things worse.
Back home, Emma would find me
some nights in the rain,
and I would try to tell her
how good it felt, standing there
for those simple, limpid
minutes rinsed of that weight
of who I was, or might be,
the whole lot washed away ...
O, the humility,
the ecstasy of it!

But how to make that last?

Just once I managed it:
that notorious morning
throned there on the beach
as if to show those toadying
noblemen my limits
or else how I was sure
the tide would stop, that I,
Canute, could command the world ...

when all I wanted was
this: to prove myself
alive – to feel, in front
of witnesses, the water
rise, to embrace its cold,
to be above nothing,
level with the sea –

and for days, for *hours*, it worked.

# Da capo

'*That's* strange', I'll think, some afternoons
and make to turn off the bathroom light
I'm all but sure I've not left on,

only to catch, for the umpteenth time,
the frosted windows splintering sunlight
like it's hitting water, and stand –

as one who needs reminding – stunned
how sometimes there's just so much light,
and how it is I never learn.

## Acknowledgements

Some of these poems first appeared in the following publications: *Assent, Granta (online), The North, Obsessed with Pipework, Oxford Poets Anthology 2002, PN Review, Poetry London, The Rialto, The Reader, Seam* and *Smiths Knoll*.

I would like to thank the following, without whose support this book would not have come into being: Trevor Donald, John Lawrence, Silvia Mulvany, Verity Meier, Katie Morgan, Helena Nelson and Nikola White. Thanks also to Sarah Blake and Hannah Westland for their work on putting this collection together, and to Don Paterson and John Stammers for coming up with the idea of the Picador Poetry Prize. I'm particularly grateful to Don Paterson for his deft and clear-eyed editing of the manuscript. And lastly, heartfelt thanks to Kate Clanchy for her kindness and wise counsel over the years.